EXPERIMENTING WI'

Ronald Stuart Thomas is seventy-nine years old. He was Vicar of Aberderon in North Wales until he retired. He is the son of a sea captain and was brought up in Holyhead and went to Bangor University. He is an intensely private man. He reads no newspapers, has no television and apart from his parishioners and his wife Mildred has little contact with the world. He is the recipient of many awards including The Queen's Gold Medal for poetry, the Cholmondely Award and the Heinemann Award of the Royal Society of Literature.

EXPERIMENTING WITH AN AMEN

BY

R. S. Thomas

PAPERMAC

First published 1986 by Macmillan London Limited

Published 1988 by
PAPERMAC
a division of Macmillan Publishers Limited
Cavaye Place London SW10 9PG
and Basingstoke

Associated companies in Auckland, Delhi, Dublin, Gaborone, Hamburg,
Harare, Hong Kong, Johannesburg, Kuala Lumpur, Lagos, Manzini,
Melbourne, Mexico City, Nairobi, New York, Singapore and Tokyo

Reprinted 1989, 1992

British Library Cataloguing in Publication Data
Thomas R. S.
    Experimenting with an amen
    I. Title
    821'.914   PR6039.H618

ISBN 0-333-46832-5

Printed in Hong Kong

Poems on pages 6, 7, 14, 19, 26, 27, 29, 30, 35, 43 and 56 have
previously been published by the Celandine Press.

CONTENTS

Formula	1
Aubade	2
Cones	3
Testimonies	4
Coming	5
A Poet	6
He and She	7
The Fly	8
Apostrophe	9
Fable	10
Hebrews 12^{29}	11
Roles	12
Gift	13
Destinations	14
Harvest End	15
The Wood	16
Biography	17
West Coast	19
Zero	20
The Bank	21
Revision	22
Similarities	24
AD 2000	25
Sarn Rhiw	26
Song	27
Ritual	28
Pardon	29
The Unvanquished	30
Calling	31
Strands	32
Countering	33
April Song	34

Gallery	35
The Window	36
Borders	37
Retirement	38
Questions	39
Looking Glass	40
The Cast	41
Court Order	42
Bequest	43
History	44
A Thicket in Lleyn	45
Nativity	46
Jerusalem	47
Confrontation	48
Moorland	49
Unposted	50
Asking	51
A Life	52
Folk Tale	53
Ystrad Fflur	54
Approaches	55
Message	56
Where?	57
This One	58
Truly	59
Retrospect	60
Andante	61
A Country	62
Their canvases are	63
Aim	64
Reply	65
Cures	66
Look Out	68
Revision	69
Fuel	70

FORMULA

And for the soul
in its bone tent, refrigerating
under the nuclear winter,
no epitaph prepared

in our benumbed language
other than the equation
hanging half-mast like the after-
birth of thought: $E = mc^2$.

AUBADE

I awoke. There was dew,
and the voice of time singing:
It is too late to begin,
you are there already.

I went to the window
as to a peep-show: There she was
all fly-wheels and pistons;
her smile invisible

as a laser. And, 'No,'
I cried, 'No' turning away
into the computed darkness
where she was waiting

for me, with art's stone
rolled aside from her belly
to reveal the place poetry had lain
with the silicon angels in attendance.

CONES

Simple in your designs,
infinite in your variations
upon them: the leaf's veins,
the shell's helix, the stars themselves
gyring down to a point
in the mind; the mind also
from that same point spiralling
outward to take in space.

Heartening that in our journeys
through time we come round not
to the same place, but recognise it
from a distance. It is the dream
we remember, that makes us say:
'We have been here before.' In
truth we are as far from it
as one side of the cone
from the other, and in between
are the false starts, the failures,
the ruins from which we climbed,
not to look down, but to feel your glance
resting on us at the next angle
of the gyre.
          God, it is not your reflections
we seek, wonderful as they are
in the live fibre; it is the possibility
of your presence at the cone's
point towards which we soar
in hope to arrive at the still
centre, where love operates
on all those frequencies
that are set up by the spinning
of two minds, the one on the other.

TESTIMONIES

The first stood up and testified to Christ:
I was made in the image of man; he unmanned me.

The second stood up: He appeared to me
in church in a stained window. I saw through him.

The third: Patient of love, I went
to him with my infirmity, and was not cured.

The fourth stood up, with between his thighs
a sword. 'He came not to bring peace' he said.

The fifth, child of his time, wasted his time
asking eternity: 'Who is my father and mother?'

So all twelve spoke, parodies of the disciples
on their way to those bone thrones from which they
    would judge others.

COMING

To be crucified
again? To be made friends
with for his jeans and beard?
Gods are not put to death

any more. Their lot now
is with the ignored.
I think he still comes
stealthily as of old,

invisible as a mutation,
an echo of what the light
said, when nobody
attended; an impression

of eyes, quicker than
to be caught looking, but taken
on trust like flowers in the
dark country towards which we go.

A POET

Disgust tempered by an exquisite
charity, wrapping life's claws
in purest linen – this man
has history to supper,
eats with a supreme tact
from the courses offered to him.

Waiting at table
are the twin graces, patience
and truth, with the candles'
irises in soft clusters
flowering on thin stalks.

Where did he come from?
Pupating against the time
he was needed, he emerged
with wings furled, unrecognised
by the pundits; has spread
them now elegantly
to dazzle, curtains drawn
with a new nonchalance
between barbarism and ourselves.

Patron without condescension
of the art, he teaches flight's
true purpose, which is,
sensitive but not too blinded
by some inner radiance, to be
in delicatest orbit about it.

HE AND SHE

When he came in, she was there.
When she looked at him
he smiled. There were lights
in time's wave breaking
on an eternal shore.

Seated at table,
no need for the fracture
of the room's silence; noiselessly
they conversed. Thoughts mingling
were lit up, gold
particles in the mind's stream.

Were there currents between them?
Why when he thought darkly
would the nerves play
at her lips' brim? What was the heart's depth?
There were fathoms in her,
too, and sometimes he crossed
them and landed and was not repulsed.

THE FLY

And the fly said: 'Nothing
to do. May as well
alight here.' No luck;
no poison. So man walked
immune down avenues
of vast promise, seeking
perfection. The fly
had it; filled in the time
flying, embroidering space
with the invisible meshwork
of flight's thread; spun rainbows
from light's spectrum. Man
worked more purposely
at his plans: immortality,
truth; killing the things would not
be killed, like time, love,
the one human, the other
one of the fly's ilk.
                What
is perfection? Anonymity's
patent? A frame fitted
for effortless success
in conveying viruses
to the curved nostril?
                I will not
be here long, but have seen
(among people) distorted
bodies, haloed with love,
shedding a radiance
where flies hung smaller
than the dust they say
man came from and to which,
I say, he will not return.

APOSTROPHE

Improvisers, he thinks,
making do with the gaps
in their knowledge; thousands of years
on the wrong track, consoling
themselves with the view by the way.
Their lives are an experiment
in deception; they increase
their lenses to keep a receding
future in sight. In arid
museums they deplore the sluggishness
of their ascent by a bone
ladder to where they took off
into space-time. They are orbited
about an unstable centre,
punishing their resources
to remain in flight.
                        There are no journeys,
I tell them. Love turns
on its own axis, as do beauty and truth,
and the wise are they
who in every generation
remain still to assess their nearness
to it by the magnitude of their shadow.

FABLE

Winged life – why
respect it? A foretaste;
heaven dwellers? But look
what we do with what

we have – the smashed decibels,
the razed cities, all
to the ticking of the unhatched
egg in a Spartan temple.

HEBREWS 12²⁹

If you had made it smaller
we would have fallen off; larger
and we would never have caught up
with our clocks. Just right
for us to know things are there
without seeing them? Forgive
us the contempt our lenses
breed in us. To be brought near
stars and microbes does us no good,
chrysalises all, that pupate
idle thoughts. We have stared and stared, and not stared
truth out, and your name has occurred
on and off with its accompanying
shadow. Who was it said: Fear
not, when fear is an ingredient
of our knowledge of you? The mistake
we make, looking deep into the fire,
is to confer features upon a presence
that is not human; to expect love
from a kiss whose only property is to consume.

ROLES

How old was he, when he asked
who he was, and receiving
no answer, asked who they
were, who projected images
of themselves on an unwilling
audience. They named him, adding
the preliminary politeness, endorsing
a claim to gentility he did not
possess. The advance towards Christian
terms was to an understanding of the significance
of repentance, courtesy put under greater
constraint; an effort to sustain the role
they insisted that he had written.
Who reaches such straits flees
to the sanctuary of his mirror for re-assurance
that he is still there, challenging the eyes
to look back into his own and not
at the third person over his shoulder.

GIFT

Some ask the world
        and are diminished
in the receiving
        of it. You gave me

only this small pool
        that the more I drink
from, the more overflows
        me with sourceless light.

DESTINATIONS

Travelling towards the light
we were waylaid by darkness;
a formless company detained us,
saying everything, meaning nothing.

'It is a conspiracy,' I said,
'of great age in revolt
against reason, against all
that would be ethereal in us.'

We looked at one another.
Was it the silence of agreement,
or the vacuum between two minds
not in contact? There is an ingredient

in thought that is its own
hindrance. Had we come all that way
to detect it? The voices combined
urging us to put our trust

in the bone's wisdom. 'Remember'
they charged us, 'the future
for which you are bound is where
you began.' Was there a counter

command? I listened as to
a tideless sea on a remote
star, and knew our direction
was elsewhere; to the light, yes,

but not such as minerals
deploy, to the brightness over
an interior horizon, which is science
transfiguring itself in love's mirror.

HARVEST END
(From the Welsh of Caledfryn)

The seasons fly;
the flowers wither;
the leaves lie
on the ground. Listen
to the sad song
of the reapers: 'Ripe
corn', as over the sea
the birds go.

Suddenly the year
ends. The wind rages;
everything in its path
breaks. Dire weather;
in front of a stick
fire, fetched from
the forest, firm and infirm
cower within doors.

The longest of lives
too soon slips by.
Careers fold and with
them good looks fade.
Spring's bloom is spent,
summer is done, too.
With a rush we come
to winter in the grave.

THE WOOD

A wood.
A man entered;
thought he knew the way
through. The old furies
attended. Did he emerge
in his right mind? The same
man? How many years
passed? Aeons? What is
the right mind? What does
'same' mean? No change of clothes
for the furies? Fast
as they are cut down
the trees grow, new
handles for axes.
There is a rumour from the heart
of the wood: brow
furrowed, mind
smooth, somebody huddles
in wide contemplation – Buddha,
Plato, Blake, Jung –
the name changes, identity
remains, pure being waiting
to be come at. Is it the self
that he mislaid? Is it why
he entered, ignoring
the warning of the labyrinth
without end? How many times
over must he begin again?

BIOGRAPHY

A life's trivia: commit them
not to the page, but to the waste-basket
of time. What was special
about you? Did you write the great
poem? Find the answer to the question:
When a little becomes much?

You made war, campaigning upon the piano
that would surrender to the television.
Were you first in the race
for the cup of silver not to be drunk
from? You ran fast and came home breathless
to the platitudes of the language.

Were you tall? Taller than you
your best tales looked over your shoulder.
There was an apple tree with a girl
under it loitering as though
for you. It was not for you, but
she accepted you for want of a better.

Among scanty possessions fear
was yours. Courage you borrowed
on short loan; set up house for the virtues
a wife brings. Venturing abroad
among the associated meannesses
you had all things in common.

Were you mobile? So was the age;
so were your standards, cheering
what yesterday was condemned
and to-morrow would be forgotten;
turning left, when you should have gone right,
to prove determinism to be in error.

And one came to your back door
all bones and in rags, asking the kiss
that would have transformed both you
and him; and you would not,
slamming it in his face, only
to find him waiting at your bed's side.

WEST COAST

Here are men
       who live at the edges
of vast space.
       Light pours on them
and they lift their faces
       to be washed by it
like children. And their minds
       are the minds of children,
shallow pools that the days
       look into as they
pass in the endless procession
       that goes nowhere.
                  They are
       spendthrifts of time, yet
always there is more of it
       than they need for the tongue's clambering
up their one story.
             Out in the fields,
against skies that are all
       blood, they erect the scarecrow
of their kind, the crossed bones
       with the flesh in tatters
upon them that have frightened
       away a lot more than the birds.

ZERO

What time is it?
　　　　Is it the hour when the servant
of Pharaoh's daughter went down
　　　　　　and found the abandoned baby
in the bulrushes? The hour
　　　　　　when Dido woke and knew Aeneas
gone from her? When Caesar
　　　　　　looked at the entrails and took
their signal for the crossing
　　　　　　of the dividing river?
　　　　　　　　　　　　Is it
that time when Aneirin
　　　　　　fetched the poem out of his side
and laid it upon the year's altar
　　　　　　for the appeasement of envious
gods?
　　　　　　It is no time
at all. The shadow falls
　　　　　　on the bright land and men
launder their minds in it, as
　　　　　　they have done century by
century to prepare themselves for the crass deed.

THE BANK

Meditating upon gold
we prick the heart on its thorns.

Yellow, yellow, yellow hair
of the spring, the poet cries,

admiring the gorse bushes
by the old stone wall. But the maiden's

hair overflows the arms
of the hero. Though you sit down

a thousand years, the echo
of the petals is inaudible

in the sunlight. Explain to me
why we use the same word

for the place that we store our money in,
and that other place where the gorse blows.

REVISION

So the catechism begins:
'Who are you?'
                  'I don't know.'
'Who gave you that ignorance?'
'It is the system that, when two people
meet, they combine to produce
the darkness in which the self
is born, a wick hungering
for its attendant flame.'
                    'What will that
do for you?'
              'Do for me? It is the echo
of a promise I am meant
to believe in.'
                'Repeat that promise.'
'Whoever believes in this fire,
although he lives, he shall die.'
                    'You
blaspheme. The promises were made
by you, not to you. What do you learn
from them?'
              'I learn there are two beings
so that, when one is present, the other
is far off. There is no room
for them both.'
              'Life's simpleton,
know this gulf you have created
can be crossed by prayer. Let me hear
if you can walk it.'
                'I have walked it.
It is called silence, and is a rope
              over an unfathomable
abyss, which goes on and on
never arriving.'

'So that your Amen
is unsaid. Know, friend, the arrival
is the grace given to maintain
your balance, the power which supplies
not the maggot of flame you desired,
that consumes the flesh, but the unseen
current between two points, coming
to song in the nerves, as in the telegraph
wires, the tighter that they are drawn.'

SIMILARITIES

I saw man staggering on his way
       with his un–necessaries. Where
was he going? He turned on me
those hurt eyes that are bold
in their weakness, bruised by a question
       he had not asked. Look,
he implied, sparing a glance
for the conjurors, the somersault
men, the mendicants with their caps brimming
       with dead leaves.
                And
the mothers were there, nursing
a dead child, and the rich endowing
a mortuary. While the youth with hair
on his chest flaunted a tin
       cross.
           Dance for me,
called the weak pipe, and the laughter
ascended to the rattle
       of a cracked drum.
             My masters,
the machine whined, putting the yawning
consciences to sleep.
           It is intolerable,
I cried. But the face
that is life's trophy stared at me
from the gallery, where it had been set
       up, so that I became silent
before it, corrected by a resemblance.

AD 2000

The gyres revolve;
man comes to the confrontation
with his terror, with the imperative
of choice. Other compulsions are shown
for what they were. Time rinses its eyes
clean. From tyranny of the hand
we are delivered to the exigencies
of freedom, to the acknowledgment
by the unlimited of its limitations.

What power shall minister to us
at the closure of the century,
of the millennia? The god,
who was Janus-faced, is eclipsed
totally by our planet, by the shadow
cast on him by contemporary
mind. Shall we continue worshipping
that mind for its halo,
its light the mirage of its radiation?

SARN RHIW

So we know
she must have said something
to him – What language,
life? Oh, what language?

Thousands of years later
I inhabit a house
whose stone is the language
of its builders. Here

by the sea they said little.
But their message to the future
was: Build well. In the fire
of an evening I catch faces

staring at me. In April,
when light quickens and clouds
thin, boneless presences
flit through my room.

Will they inherit me
one day? What certainties
have I to hand on
like the punctuality

with which, at the moon's
rising, the bay breaks
into a smile as though meaning
were not the difficulty at all?

SONG

Round and round;
take my hand, dance
at the grave's edge, dance
like an angel on a pin's
head — see you
after the explosion.

And I, an old stump
cast up on time's
shore . . . Hush, the children
will hear you. I fill
their stockings with coins
that are the leaves

of a failed culture. Waiting
under the mistletoe
cluster I saw peace
stand, and no-one willing
to go up and kiss her
for laughing at her old-fashioned clothes.

RITUAL

Not international
renown, but international
vocabulary, the macaronics
of time: μοῖρα, desiderium,
brad, la vida
breve, despair – I am the bone
on which all have beaten out
their message to the mind
that would soar. Faithful
in translation, its ploy was to evade
my resources. It saw
me dance through the Middle
Ages, and wrote its poetry
with quilled pen. What
so rich as the language
to which the priests
buried me? They have exchanged
their vestments for white coats,
working away in their bookless
laboratories, ministrants
in that ritual beyond words
which is the Last Sacrament of the species.

PARDON

I began by praising the beetle,
time's brooch on the earth's tunic.

I grew bolder. The slug's glair
was pearly in the dawn's jeweller's shop.

I looked at the sky for approval:
Keep going. The fox was a bush

on fire, the ground holy,
littered though it was with the dove's ashes.

And homo sapiens, that cracked mirror,
mending himself again and again like a pool?

Who threw the stone? I forgave him his surface
in the name of the unseen troubler of his depths.

THE UNVANQUISHED

And courage shall give way
to despair and despair
to suffering and suffering
shall end in death. But you
who are not free to choose
what you suffer can choose
your response. Farmers I
knew, born to the ills
of their kind, scrubbed bare
by the weather, suffocating
with phlegm; all their means gone
to buy their consumptive son
the profession his body
could not sustain. Proudly
they lived, watching the spirit,
diamond-faceted, crumble
to the small, hard, round, dry
stone that humanity
chokes on. When they died, it
was bravely, close up under the rain-hammered
rafters, never complaining.

CALLING

The telephone is the fruit
of the tree of the knowledge
of good and evil. We may call
everyone up on it but God.

To do that is to declare
that he is far off. Dialling
zero is nothing other
than the negation of his presence.

So many times I have raised
the receiver, listening to
that smooth sound that is technology's
purring; and the temptation

has come to experiment
with the code which would put
me through to the divine
snarl at the perimeter of such tameness.

STRANDS

It was never easy.
There was a part of us,
trailing uterine
memories, would have lapsed
back into Eden, the mindless
place. There was a part,
masochistic, terrifying itself
with a possibility – infinite
freedom in confrontation
with infinite love; the idea
of a balance, where we should come
to be weighed, lifting horrified
eyes to a face that was more
than human. And a part
amenable to the alternatives:
nature, mechanism, evolution,
bearers of a torch kindled
to illuminate primaeval
caves that has become electric,
the probing searchlight piercing
beyond the galaxies, shocking
the manipulator of it with its ability
to discover nothing, the ultimate
hole the intrepid reason
has dug for itself.
                    Must we
draw back? Is there a far side
to an abyss, and can our wings
take us there? Or is man's
meaning in the keeping of himself
afloat over seventy thousand
fathoms, tacking against winds
coming from no direction,
going in no direction?

COUNTERING

Then there is the clock's
commentary, the continuing
prose that is the under-current
of all poetry. We listen
to it as, on a desert island,
men do to the subdued
music of their blood in a shell.

Then take my hand that is
of the bone the island
is made of, and looking at
me say what time it is
on love's face, for we have
no business here other than
to disprove certainties the clock knows.

APRIL SONG

Withdrawing from the present,
wandering a past that is alive
in books only. In love
with women, outlasted

by their smiles; the richness
of their apparel puts
the poor in perspective.
The brush dipped in blood

and the knife in art
have preserved their value.
Smouldering times: sacked
cities, incinerable hearts,

and the fledgling God
tipped out of his high
nest into the virgin's lap
by the incorrigible cuckoo.

GALLERY

The stillness of paintings!
Move stealthily so
as not to disturb.

They are not asleep.
They keep watch on
our taste. It is not they

are being looked at
but we by faces
which over the centuries

keep their repose. Such eyes
they have as, steadily,
while crowds come and

crowds go, burn on
with art's crocus flame
in their enamelled sockets.

THE WINDOW

Say he is any man
anywhere set before the shop window
of life, full of comestibles
and jewels; to put out his hand
is to come up against
glass; to break it is
to injure himself.
                    Shall he turn
poet and acquire them
in the imagination, gospeller
and extol himself for his abstention
from them?
                    What if he is not
called? I would put the manufacturers
there. Let them see the eyes
staring in, be splashed with the blood
of the shop-breakers; let them live
on the poet's diet, on the pocket-money
of the priest.
                    I see the blinds
going down in Europe, over the
whole world: the rich with everything to
sell, the poor with nothing to buy it with.

BORDERS

Somewhere beyond time's
curve civilisation lifted
its glass rim. There was
a pretence of light

for nations to walk by
through the dark wood, where history
wintered. Following I came
to the foretold frontier

where with a machine's
instinct the guns' nostrils
flared at the blooms held out
to them by the flower people.

RETIREMENT

I have crawled out at last
far as I dare on to a bough
of country that is suspended
between sky and sea.

From what was I escaping?
There is a rare peace here,
though the aeroplanes buzz me,
reminders of that abyss,

deeper than sea or sky, civilisation
could fall into. Strangers
advance, inching their way
out, so that the branch bends

further away from the scent
of the cloud blossom. Must
I console myself
with reflections? There are

times even the mirror
is misted as by one breathing
over my shoulder. Clinging
to my position, witnessing

the seasonal migrations,
I must try to content
myself with the perception
that love and truth have

no wings, but are resident
like me here, practising
their sub-song quietly in the face
of the bitterest of winters.

QUESTIONS

She should put off modesty
with her shift. Who said that?
Should one, then, put off belief
with one's collar? The girl enters
the bed, enters the man's
arms to be clasped between sheets
against the un-love that is all around.

The priest lies down alone
face to face with the darkness
that is the nothing from which nothing
comes. 'Love' he protests, 'love'
in spiritual copulation
with a non–body, hearing the echoes
dying away, languishing under the owl's curse.

What is a bed for? Is there no repose
in the small hours? No proofing of sleep's
stuff against the fretting of stars, thoughts?
Tell me, then, after the night's toil
of loving or praying, is there nothing
to do but to rise tired and be made
away with, yawning, into the day's dream?

LOOKING GLASS

There is a game I play
with a mirror, approaching
it when I am not there,
as though to take by surprise

the self that is my familiar. It
is in vain. Like one eternally
in ambush, fast or slow
as I may raise my head, it raises

its own, catching me in the act,
disarming me by acquaintance,
looking full into my face as often
as I try looking at it askance.

THE CAST

'Look up' they said
            at the rehearsal
of the film. 'Higher, higher' –
(preparing for the monster)
and the screaming began,
            the nightmare
from which there is no waking.
                        Ah, vertical God,
whose altitudes are the mathematics
            that confound us,
what is thought but the mind's
            scream as it hurtles
in free-fall down your immense
side, hurrying everywhere,
arriving nowhere but at the precipitousness
            of your presence?
                        We weigh
nothing. Is it that you assess
            us by our ability,
upside down as we are,
to look forward to averages
            that you have left behind?

COURT ORDER

'My good fool' he
    who was a king
said, 'come hither, perch
    at my side; challenge
me to make some sport
    with this word "Love" '. I
did so, and was tumbled
    into the world without
cap and bells, to end
    up on a hard
shoulder, not laughing
    with the rest who knew
that Friday, it being April,
    was All Fools' Day.

BEQUEST

Wanting peace we were misled
by a dead nation's counsel
to prepare for war. Thinking love
would survive an instruction
in violence we took ourselves back
to a dark school, terrified
ourselves with our own propaganda.

As Germans their nostrils
with bad smells, we inoculated
ourselves with the poison factories
in our meadows. Our scientists
had white coats, vestments
these of a clandestine ritual.

Somewhere from under an old
dustbin lid you will have emerged
for the re-assembling of the species.
We have left you nothing
but the consequences of our refusal
to sit down by the still pool
in the mind, waiting for the unknown
visitant's quickening of its surface.

HISTORY

In the morning among colonnades
a Greek radiance. At mid-day
time stood vertically between them
and the answer that was not
far off. At mid-day somewhere else
time was appalled, seeing its shadow
dislocated by a body the issues
of which were for the conversion
of a soldier. Civilisation rounded
towards its afternoon, the languid siesta
of brawn and muscle. The monks' pupils
contracted through peering into
the reformed light. A vessel took off
into navigable waters to discover how mutinous
was the truth. As the sun went down
the lights came on in a million
laboratories, as the scientists attempted
to turn the heart's darkness into intellectual day.

A THICKET IN LLEYN

I was no tree walking.
I was still. They ignored me,
the birds, the migrants
on their way south. They re-leafed
the trees, budding them
with their notes. They filtered through
the boughs like sunlight,
looked at me from three feet
off, their eyes blackberry bright,
not seeing me, not detaching me
from the withies, where I was
caged and they free.
                    They would have perched
on me, had I had nourishment
in my fissures. As it was,
they netted me in their shadows,
brushed me with sound, feathering the arrows
of their own bows, and were gone,
leaving me to reflect on the answer
to a question I had not asked.
'A repetition in time of the eternal
I AM.' Say it. Don't be shy.
Escape from your mortal cage
in thought. Your migrations will never
be over. Between two truths
there is only the mind to fly with.
Navigate by such stars as are not
leaves falling from life's
deciduous tree, but spray from the fountain
of the imagination, endlessly
replenishing itself out of its own waters.

NATIVITY

The moon is born
and a child is born,
lying among white clothes
as the moon among clouds.

They both shine, but
the light from the one
is abroad in the universe
as among broken glass.

JERUSALEM

A city — its name
keeps it intact. Don't
touch it. Let the muezzin's
cry, the blood call

of the Christian, the wind
from sources desiccated
as the spirit drift over
its scorched walls. Time

devourer of its children
chokes here on the fact
it is in high places love
condescends to be put to death.

CONFRONTATION

And there was the serpent
running like water
but more quietly with no desire
to bicker. They see us
with smooth eye; what is man
in a snake's world? And if
we would come too close,
they strike us as painfully
as the truth.
                    It is no part
of divine mind to repudiate
its reflections. We must exchange
stare for stare, looking
into that eye as into a dark
crystal, asking if Eden
is where we must continually
seek to charm evil by playing
to it, knowing that it is deaf.

MOORLAND

It is beautiful and still;
        the air rarefied
as the interior of a cathedral

expecting a presence. It is where, also,
        the harrier occurs,
materialising from nothing, snow-

soft, but with claws of fire,
        quartering the bare earth
for the prey that escapes it;

hovering over the incipient
        scream, here a moment, then
not here, like my belief in God.

UNPOSTED

Dear friend unknown,
why send me your poems?
We are brothers, I admit;
but they are no good.
I see why you wrote them,
but why send them? Why not
bury them, as a cat its faeces?
You confuse charity and art.
They have not equal claims,
though the absence of either
will smell more or less the same.

I use my imagination:
I see a cramped hand gripping
a bent pen, or, worse perhaps,
it was with your foot you wrote.
You wait in an iron bed
for my reply. My letter
could be the purse of gold
you pay your way with past
the giant, Despair.
                    I lower my standards
and let truth hit me squarely
between the eyes. 'These are great
poems', I write, and see heaven's
slums with their rags flying,
cripples brandishing their crutches,
and the one, innocent of scansion,
who knows charity is short
and the poem for ever, suffering
my dark lie with all the blandness
with which the round moon suffers an eclipse.

ASKING

Did I see religion,
its hand in the machine's,
trying to smile as the grip
tightened? Did I hear money

arguing out of the tree's
branches, shadowing
the world, about the love
at its root? How beautiful

in a world like this
are the feet of the peace
makers upon the mountains
risen out of our own molehills?

A LIFE

Lived long; much fear, less
courage. Bottom in love's school
of his class; time's reasons
too far back to be known.
Good on his knees, yielding,
vertical, to petty temptations.
A mouth thoughts escaped
from unfledged. Where two
were company, he the unwanted
third. A Narcissus tortured
by the whisperers behind
the mirror. Visionary only
in his perception of an horizon
beyond the horizon. Doubtful
of God, too pusillanimous
to deny him. Saving his face
in verse from the humiliations prose
inflicted on him. One of life's
conscientious objectors, conceding
nothing to the propaganda of death
but a compulsion to volunteer.

FOLK TALE

Prayers like gravel
      flung at the sky's
window, hoping to attract
         the loved one's
attention. But without
      visible plaits to let
down for the believer
        to climb up,
to what purpose open
      that far casement?
        I would
have refrained long since
      but that peering once
through my locked fingers
I thought that I detected
      the movement of a curtain.

YSTRAD FFLUR
(Strata Florida)

I hardly knew him.
The place was old,
ruins of an ideal in chaste
minds. Rows of graves
signalled their disappointment.
Time, I said. Place, he replied,
not contradicting.
          Had we found
what we sought, for him
somewhere, for me when
to listen to a mossed voice
beyond our dimensions?
Where are the twelve gates?
I wondered, looking at the low
archway through which we had come.
Had the years left us
only this one? Must masculine thoughts
once more be tonsured?
          I am
a musician, the voice said.
I play on the bone keys in an audience's
absence. The light twitched,
as though at the blinking
of an immense eyelid; the foliage
rippled in shadowy applause.
We regarded one another,
neither wanting to be first
to propose. Is every proposal
a renunciation? Was our return
mutual to where the machine offered
its accelerating alternatives
to the noon-day of the soul?

APPROACHES

We began by being very close.
Moving nearer I found
he was further off, presence
being replaced by shadow;

the nearer the light, the larger
the shadow. Imagine the torment
of the discovery that it was growing
small. Is there a leak somewhere

in the mind that would comprehend
him? Not even to be able to say,
pointing: Here Godhead was spilled.
I had a belief once that even

a human being left his stain
in places where he had occurred.
Now it is all clinical light
pouring into the interstices

where mystery could linger
questioning credentials of the divine
fossil, sterilising our thought
for its launching into its own outer space.

MESSAGE

A message from God
delivered by a bird
at my window, offering friendship.
Listen. Such language!
Who said God was without
speech? Every word an injection
to make me smile. Meet me,
it says, to-morrow here
at the same time and you will remember
how wonderful to-day
was: no pain, no worry;
irrelevant the mystery, if
unsolved. I gave you the X-ray
eye for you to use not
to prospect, but to discover
the un-malignancy of love's
growth. You were a patient, too,
anaesthetised on truth's table
with life operating on you
with a green scalpel. Meet me, I say,
to-morrow and I will sing it for you
all over again, when you have come to.

WHERE?

Where to turn without turning
to stone? From the one side
history's Medusa stares,
from the other one love

on its cross. While the heart
fills not with light
from the mind, but with the shadow
too much of such light casts.

THIS ONE

Sometimes a shadow passed
between him and the light.
Sometimes a light showed itself
in the darkness beyond. Could
it be? The strong angels wrestled
and were not disposed to give
him the verdict. Are there journeys
without destinations? The animals
paused and became gargoyles
beside the way. And this one,
standing apart to confer
with the eternal, was he blamed
for reaction? There is always
laughter out of the speeding
vehicles for the man
who is still, half-way though he be
in a better direction. From receding
horizons he has withdrawn
his mind for greater repose
on an inner perspective,
where love is the bridge between
thought and time. Consumers
of distance at vast cost,
what do they know of the green
twig with which he divines,
where life balances excess
of death, the bottomless
water that is the soul's glass?

TRULY

No, I was not born
to refute Hume, to write
the first poem with no
noun. My gift was

for evasion, taking
cover at the approach
of greatness, as of
ill-fame. I looked truth

in the eye, and was not
abashed at discovering
it squinted. I fasted
at import's table, so had

an appetite for the banal,
the twelve baskets full left
over after the turning
of the little into so much.

RETROSPECT

As they became
cleverer, they became worse —
So history publishes
its contempt for the scholars

who can't spell. One thing
I remember: There was
a man time should have
bowed down to: bones of a bird,

great brain, whose argument broke
on the big fist; while a girl wept
her confetti tears,
bellowing to be deflowered.

ANDANTE

Masters, you who would initiate
me in discourse, apostrophising
the deity: O Thou, to Whom . . .
out of date three hundred
years. The atoms translate
into their own terms, burnishing
the dust, converting it
to a presence, a movement of light
on the room's wall, a smile quickening
and going out as the clouds
canter. Inhabitants of a flower
they fix that gaze on us
which is without focus, but compels
the attention, mesmerising us until
we are adrift on its scent's timelessness.
The huskiness of an emotion!
Can molecules feel? There is the long sigh
from the shore, the wave clearing
its throat to address us, requiring
no answer than the due
we give these things that share
the world with us, that compose
the world: an ever-renewed
symphony to be listened to
admiringly, even as we perform
it on whatever instruments
the generations put into our hands.

A COUNTRY

It is nowhere,
          and I am familiar
with it as one is
with a song.
             I know its background,
               the terraces
of cloud that are the hanging gardens
              of the imagination.
No sun
          rises there, so there is no sun
to set. It is the mind
suffuses it with a light
         that is without
           shadows.
                 Invisible fountains
play, though their skirts
are of silk.
           And who lives there,
you ask, who walks
its unmetalled highways?
           It is a people
who pay their taxes
          in poetry; who repair broken
names; who wear the past
as a button-hole at their children's
           marriage with what is to be.

THEIR CANVASES ARE

full of the timeless faces
of their kind, gazing out
at a distance that is empty
of our inventions and serene

so. The trees are dark
flames, burning in the Florentine
weather in answer to
the need of the blind hand

for form, kindling nothing
but the imagination, for
the earth that produced
these was fertile of

worse things: our shadows,
for instance. Fortunate
people, foreseeing so much
on the horizon, but never ourselves coming.

AIM

A voice out of the land –
animal, vegetable, mineral –
'The pain, the beauty – Why, why, why?
Tell me the truth, give me
understanding.'
          And the rose
wastes its syllables; the rock fixes
its stare; the stoat sips
at the brimmed rabbit.
             And one,
Ieuan Morgan, his mind
in a sling, goes on his way
past the crouched chapel,
its doors' barrels levelled
on him out of the last
century, neither knowing nor caring
whether he is a marked man.

REPLY

Do the wheels praise,
          humming to themselves
as they proceed in unnecessary
          directions? Do the molecules
bow down? Before what cradle
          do the travellers from afar,
strontium and plutonium, hold out
          their thin gifts? What
is missing from the choruses
          of bolts and rivets, as they prepare
for the working of their expensive
          miracle high in the clerestories
of blind space? What anthem have our computers
          to insert into the vacuum caused
by the break in transmission
          of the song upon Patmos?

CURES

'We sat under a tree
at the season when elms
put forth their leaves. It was then
Guillemette Benet said to me:
"My poor friend, my poor friend,
the soul is nothing
but blood." '*

                    So the deposition
at Foix. Inquisitor,
what would you have the soul
be to escape the rigour
of your laundering? Your Christ
died for you; for whom
would you have these die?
No answer. He has withdrawn
iron-faced into the silence
from which history resurrects
everything but our reasons.

Meanwhile a few leagues
to the west, like a suppuration
of grace, the soiled fountain
plays, where the scientists gather
bacteria. Their claims are refuted
by the virgin smile on the face
of the water. Holy Church
has become wise, recognising
the anaemic soul is no substitute
for the bone's need.

*From *Montaillou* by Emmanuel le Roy Ladurie, translated by Barbara Bra'

                              And the mind,
then, weary of the pilgrimages
to its horizons – is there no spring of thought
adjacent to it, where it can be
dipped, so that emerging but
once in ten thousand times,
freed of its crutches, is sufficient
testimony to the presence in it
of a power other than its own?

LOOK OUT

At the dance of the dust,
          at the recital
of flies, the master of ceremonies
is the scarecrow, brandishing
          his baton. Is this
evening-dress? we ask,
          admiring his shirt-front
of fresh straw.
                    'Pouf' says the wind,
'by his lack of expression
          he conducts nothing,
not even himself.'
                    'Are the crossed sticks
          where I must perch?' the dove
wonders.
          And history: 'I have wasted
                    all my time
in ascending him, but
          there is no view from the top.'

REVISION

Heaven affords
      unlimited accommodation
to the simple-minded.
                    Pardon,
hymn–writers, if levity deputises
      for an Amen. Too much
has depended on the exigencies
      of rhyme. You never
improved on 'odd' as the antiphon
      to a heavenly father.
                        Tell
me, is truth's victory followed
      by an armistice?
                  How many
of man's prayers assume
      an eavesdropping God?
                  A bishop
      called for an analysis
of the bread and wine. I being
      no chemist play my recording
of his silence over
      and over to myself only.

FUEL

And the machines say, laughing
up what would have been sleeves
in the old days: 'We are at
your service.' 'Take us', we cry,

'to the places that are far off
from yourselves.' And so they do
at a price that is the alloy in
the thought that we can do without them.